Copyright © 2019 by Joy Church International

All rights reserved. No part of this publication may be reproduced, distributed, or transmitted in any form or by any means, including photocopying, recording, or other electronic or mechanical methods, without the prior written permission of the publisher, except in the case of brief quotations embodied in critical reviews and certain other non-commercial uses permitted by copyright law. For permission requests, write to the publisher, addressed "Attention: Permissions Coordinator," at the address below.

Joy Church
P.O. Box 247
Mount Juliet, TN 37121
www.joychurch.net

Printed in the United States of America

Publisher's Cataloging-in-Publication data
Frease, Jim.
Winning with Wisdom: Pearls of Wisdom for Your Next Right Decision - Volume Four / Jim Frease.
p. 196
ISBN 978-0-9983918-5-4
1. Motivational 2. Inspirational. 3. Christian Living.

First Edition
First Printing 2019

To Keith, my son in the faith.
Thank you for helping bring my books alive.
I love and believe in you!

Winning with Wisdom

Wisdom is the principal thing.
Therefore, get wisdom.

The Bible tells us, "Wise men store up knowledge..." (Proverbs 10:14 NKJV). Did you know that the quality of your life is determined by the quality of your decisions, and the quality of your decisions is determined by the quality of information you store up? Therefore, if we truly desire a better quality of life, we must make better quality decisions with better quality information.

This little "nugget"-style book is designed to invest in your storehouse of knowledge so you can eventually enjoy a better quality of life. As you peruse the pages of this book, don't be overwhelmed by the quantity of information, but rather focus on the quality of change.

Remember this: invest in knowledge now, and it will compound in wisdom later!

You are not a loser. You are a chooser! *Winning with Wisdom* is designed to help you make your next right decision.

- JIM FREASE

Table of contents

INSPIRATION — 10

PERSPECTIVE — 36

ADULTING — 66

SPEAKING LIFE — 98

MINISTRY — 130

DEVOTION — 164

YOU CAN'T BE DEFEATED IF YOU CAN'T BE DISCOURAGED.

INSPIRATION

Don't run from your Red Seas.
They are the road to your victory
and the demise of your enemies.

To run from your mountain is
to run from your own maturity.

INSPIRATION

Tough people last.
Tough times don't.

Many times, the greatest pressure to quit comes right before manifested victory.

INSPIRATION

Don't let failure be an excuse to not try again.

Champions are not people who don't fail.
Champions are people who don't quit.

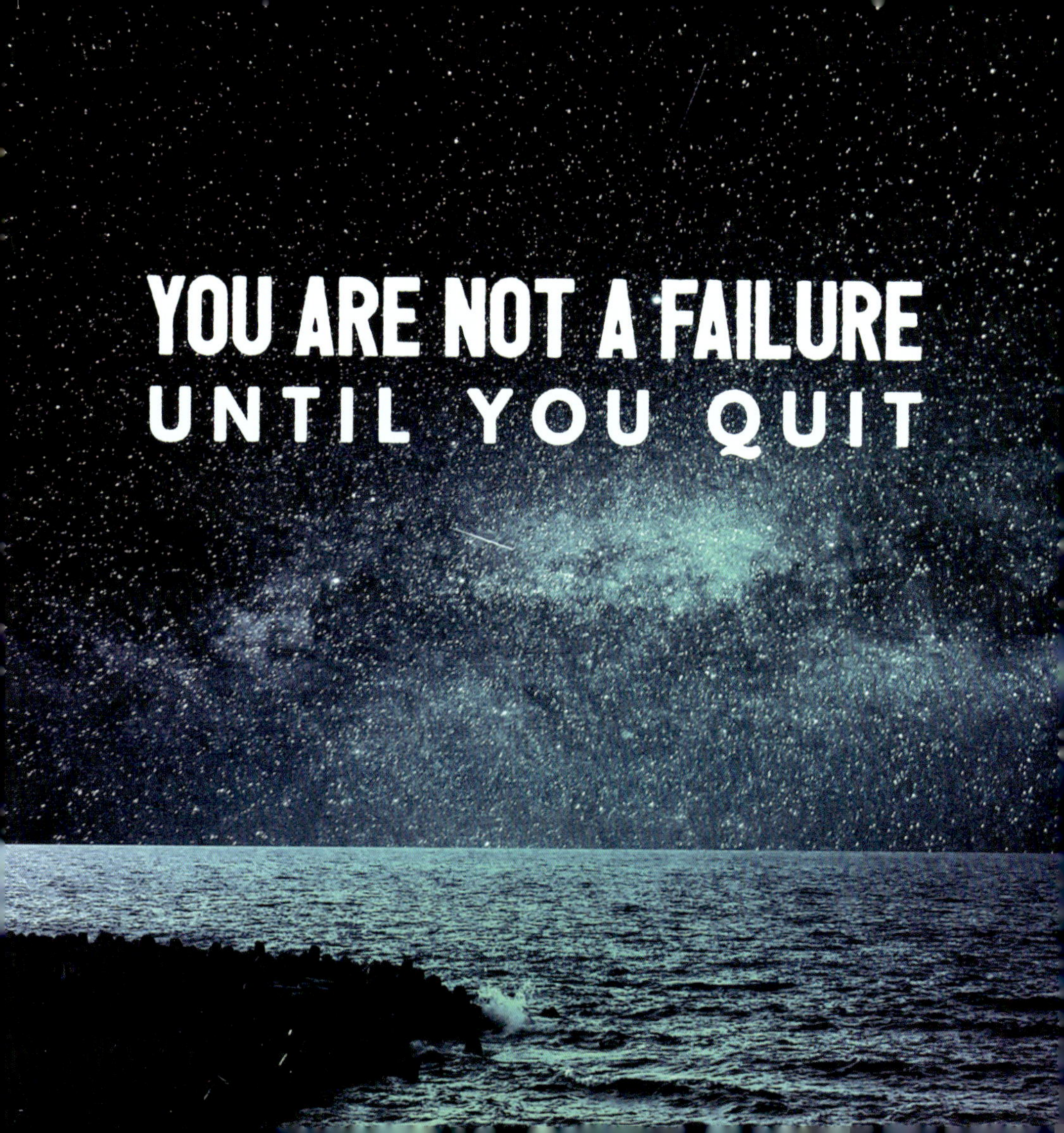
YOU ARE NOT A FAILURE
UNTIL YOU QUIT

INSPIRATION

Let yesterday's conquests
remind you of God's faithfulness today.

If God has brought you this far,
He'll take you the rest of the way.

INSPIRATION

Never race to tomorrow
without stopping to taste today.

Enjoy the journey right where you are,
on the way to where you're going.

INSPIRATION

Miracles occur when divine orchestration meets human cooperation.

One ordinary act of obedience can result in an extraordinary act of God.

INSPIRATION

Sow your life into the success of others,
and God will take care of your success.

When your life is over,
the only people who will remember you
are those whose lives you contributed to.

INSPIRATION

To find a better tomorrow,
you must be willing
to leave your comfort zone today.

When you step out in boldness,
God will meet you with His power.

INSPIRATION

When doing small things, think about big things.
Then, small things become meaningful things.

Little sacrifices that no one sees
produce great successes that everyone sees.

DILIGENCE IS DOING LITTLE THINGS FOR A LONG TIME UNTIL IT MAKES A BIG DIFFERENCE.

INSPIRATION

If you're waiting for the perfect time, you'll never fulfill your destiny.

Start broke, start weak, start wherever you are. But, for the love of God, start!

INSPIRATION

To create something you've never had,
you must do something you've never done.

When was the last time
you did something for the first time?
If it's been a long time, then it's about time.

INSPIRATION

You have to choose
what you have been chosen for.

Every decision you make will take you either closer to or further away from your destiny.

YOU DON'T SEE LIFE AS IT IS.
YOU SEE LIFE AS YOU ARE.

PERSPECTI

PERSPECTIVE

Your life will always go in the direction
of your predominant thoughts.

If you can't control what you think,
it will be very hard to control what you do.

your thoughts
MATTER

PERSPECTIVE

Your thoughts determine your feelings.
Your feelings determine your actions.
Your actions determine your life.

You can't think failure and have success.
You can't think sickness and have healing.
You can't think depression and have joy.
You can't think worry and have peace.

you can't have **NEGATIVE THOUGHTS** *and live a* **POSITIVE LIFE.**

PERSPECTIVE

Learn to celebrate your progress.

You may not have arrived yet,
but at least you've left.

DON'T FOCUS ON HOW FAR YOU HAVE LEFT TO GO.
FOCUS ON HOW FAR YOU'VE COME.

PERSPECTIVE

You should always expect
to be delivered from your problem.

Minimize your problem
and magnify the promise
that will deliver you from your problem.

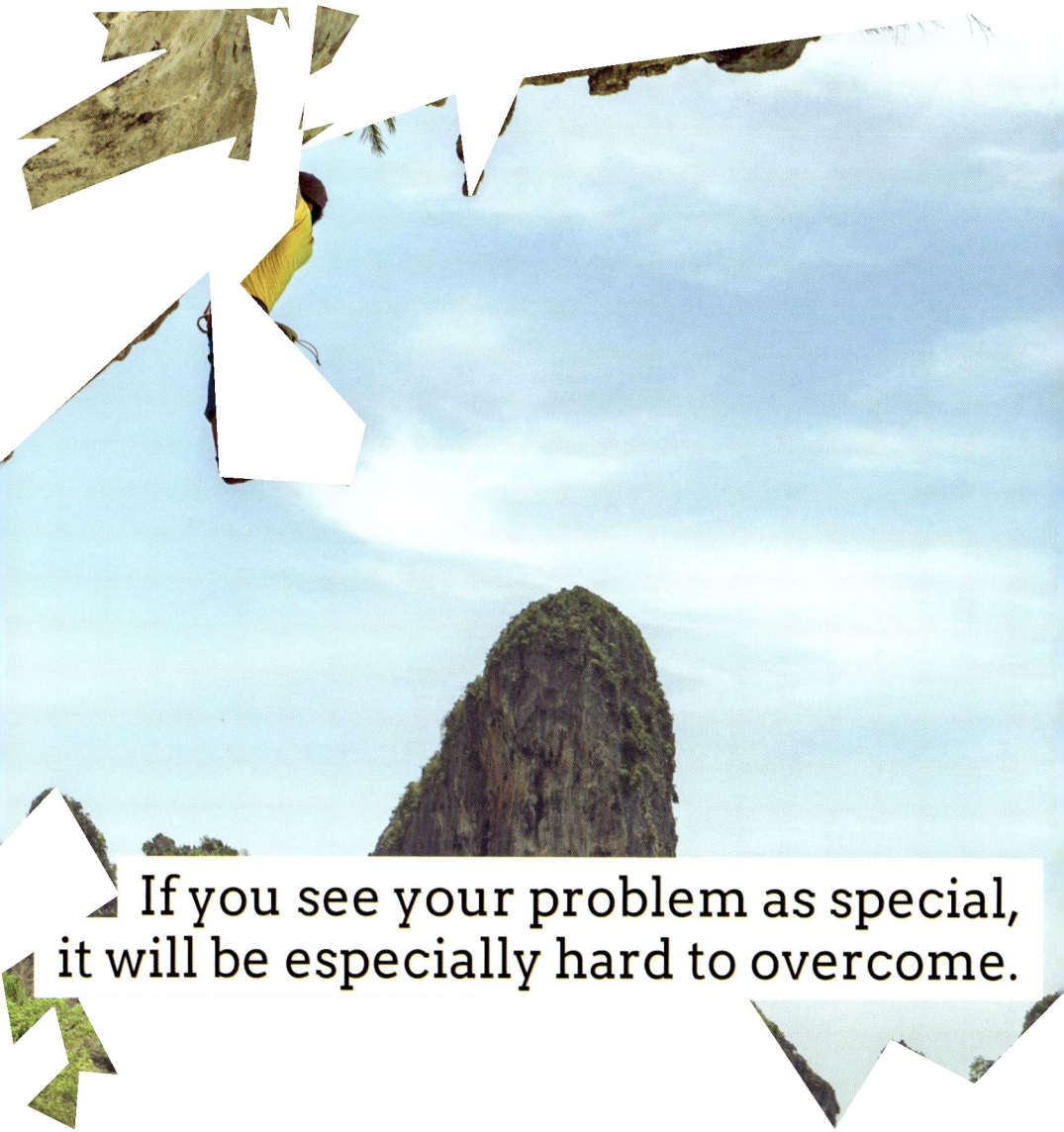

If you see your problem as special, it will be especially hard to overcome.

PERSPECTIVE

Look for silver linings in clouds of crisis.

When we change the way we look at things, the things we look at change.

BEFORE YOUR CIRCUMSTANCES CAN CHANGE, YOU MUST CHANGE HOW YOU SEE THEM.

PERSPECTIVE

You can't always control what happens to you,
but you can control how you frame it.

Learn to be thankful
for what *didn't* happen to you.

IT'S EASY TO LAUGH

WHEN EVERYTHING IS GOING RIGHT.

IT'S IMPORTANT TO LAUGH

WHEN EVERYTHING IS GOING WRONG.

PERSPECTIVE

Life is 10% what happens to you
and 90% how you react to it.

How you perceive life will determine
what you receive in life.

IT'S NOT WHAT HAPPENS TO YOU
BUT HOW YOU
PERCEIVE IT
THAT DEFINES YOUR LIFE.

PERSPECTIVE

Don't look at what you're going through.
Look at what you're going to.

The devil's assignment is to
get you to take your eyes off the seed in you
and get your eyes on the storm around you.

WHAT GETS YOUR ATTENTION GETS YOU.

PERSPECTIVE

It's not happy people who are grateful.
It's grateful people who are happy.

One of the devil's biggest lies is
"the one thing you don't have is the one thing
that will make you happy."

GRATITUDE TURNS WHATEVER WE HAVE INTO ENOUGH.

PERSPECTIVE

Never complain about what you don't have
when you're not using what you do have.

It's okay to desire more,
but you must learn to be content where you are.

| DON'T LET THE BLESSINGS YOU WANT
ROB YOU OF THE BLESSINGS YOU HAVE.

PERSPECTIVE

God is a restorer.

There's more where that came from!

Don't focus on what you lost. Focus on the **GOD** who supplied it in the first place!

PERSPECTIVE

Replaying an event in your mind will never change the outcome.

Never let yesterday's memories become bigger than today's dreams.

That was then

This is NOW

PERSPECTIVE

The only thing you can do about your past is get over it.

Build on past successes,
learn from past failures,
but move on!

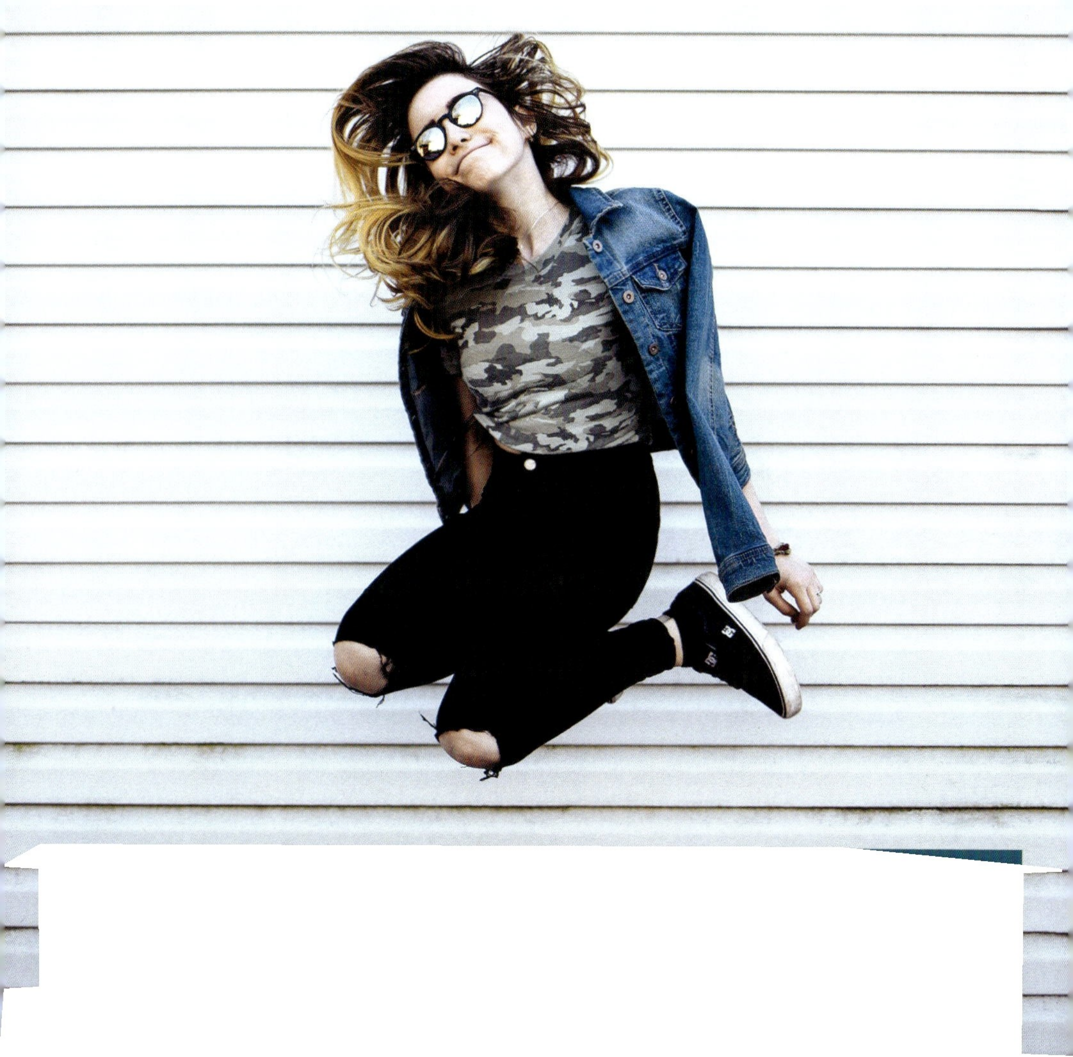

PERSPECTIVE

The attitude you have is the one you've chosen.

It's not fake it 'til you make it.
It's choose it or you'll lose it!

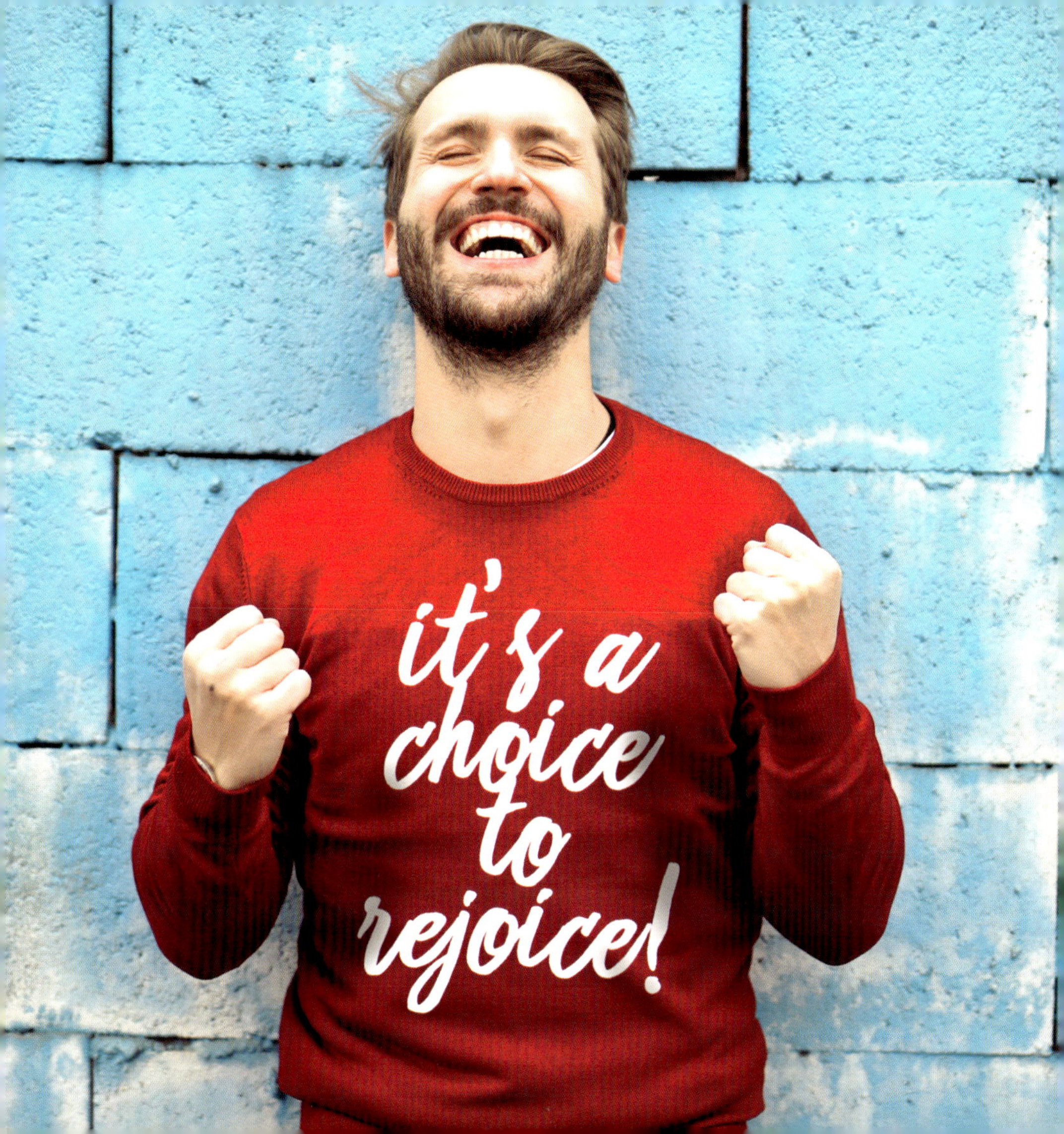
it's a choice to rejoice!

AGE IS NOT A GUARANTEE FOR MATURITY. IT'S ONLY AN OPPORTUNITY FOR MATURITY.

ADULTING

ADULTING

Enthusiasm will get you started.
Discipline will keep you going.

Discipline is simply
doing what you don't want to do
so you can do what *do* want to do.

Ability is useless without the discipline to point it in the right direction.

ADULTING

To make no decision out of fear is to make the wrong decision.

Indecision is the breeding ground for a wasted life.

THE LONGER YOU PUT SOMETHING OFF,

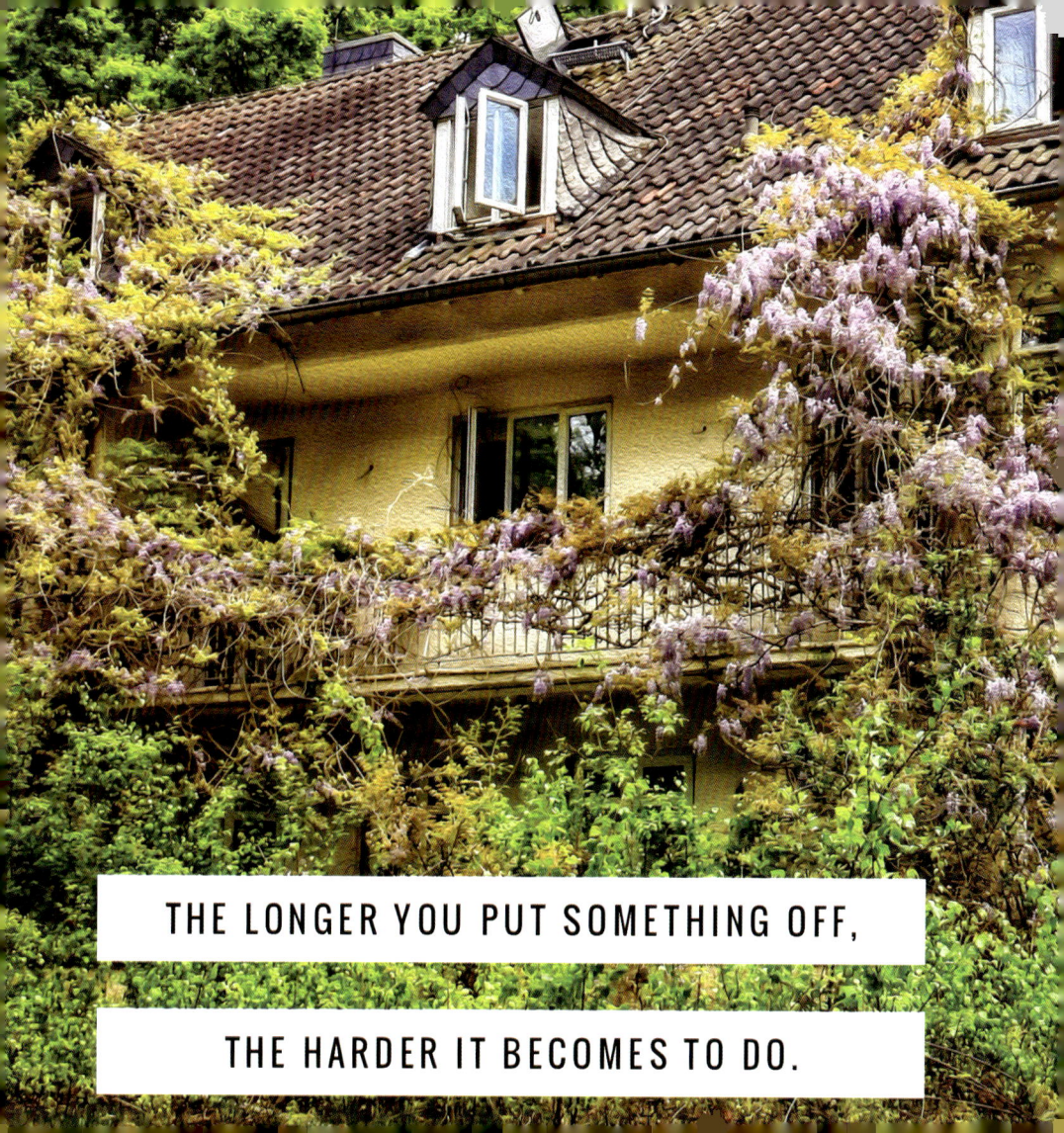

THE HARDER IT BECOMES TO DO.

ADULTING

There's more to this life than this life.

You must learn to live for eternity
and not next weekend.

WHAT YOU TALK ABOUT ALL THE TIME
REVEALS WHAT YOUR GOD IS

ADULTING

The sooner you learn
to submit to imperfect people,
the sooner you'll be promoted.

You are not ready to lead
until you can let those in authority
be human and still respect them.

BY SUBMITTING TO AUTHORITY NOW, YOU PREPARE YOURSELF TO BE IN AUTHORITY LATER.

ADULTING

You can either play the victim or the victor.
The role you continually play
will be the role you eventually become.

You can either get bitter or get better.

WHAT IS MORE IMPORTANT TO YOU?
SYMPATHY OR SUCCESS?

ADULTING

If you don't hate debt, you'll tolerate it. What you tolerate, you cannot change.

If your outgo is greater than your income, then your upkeep will be your downfall.

SPENDING MONEY YOU DON'T HAVE IS STEALING FROM YOURSELF.

ADULTING

We live in a generation that says,
"Why pay cash when you can make payments?"
But plastic prosperity is not true prosperity.

Unwise debt raises your standard of stuff
but lowers your standard of living.

"I WANT" IS BETTER THAN "I OWE."

ADULTING

How you handle little
will be how you handle more.

When you buy things you can't afford,
you're telling God that you're not content
with Him or His provision.

YOU MUST BE THANKFUL FOR PROVISION BEFORE YOU GET TO ABUNDANCE.

ADULTING

If your relationships are dysfunctional, your life will be too.

Sometimes, you must decide between your friends and your future.

your relationship decisions ARE AMONG YOUR MOST IMPORTANT DECISIONS.

ADULTING

Focus less on finding the right person,
and focus more on becoming the right person.

God entrusts His finest blessings
to those who know how to handle them.

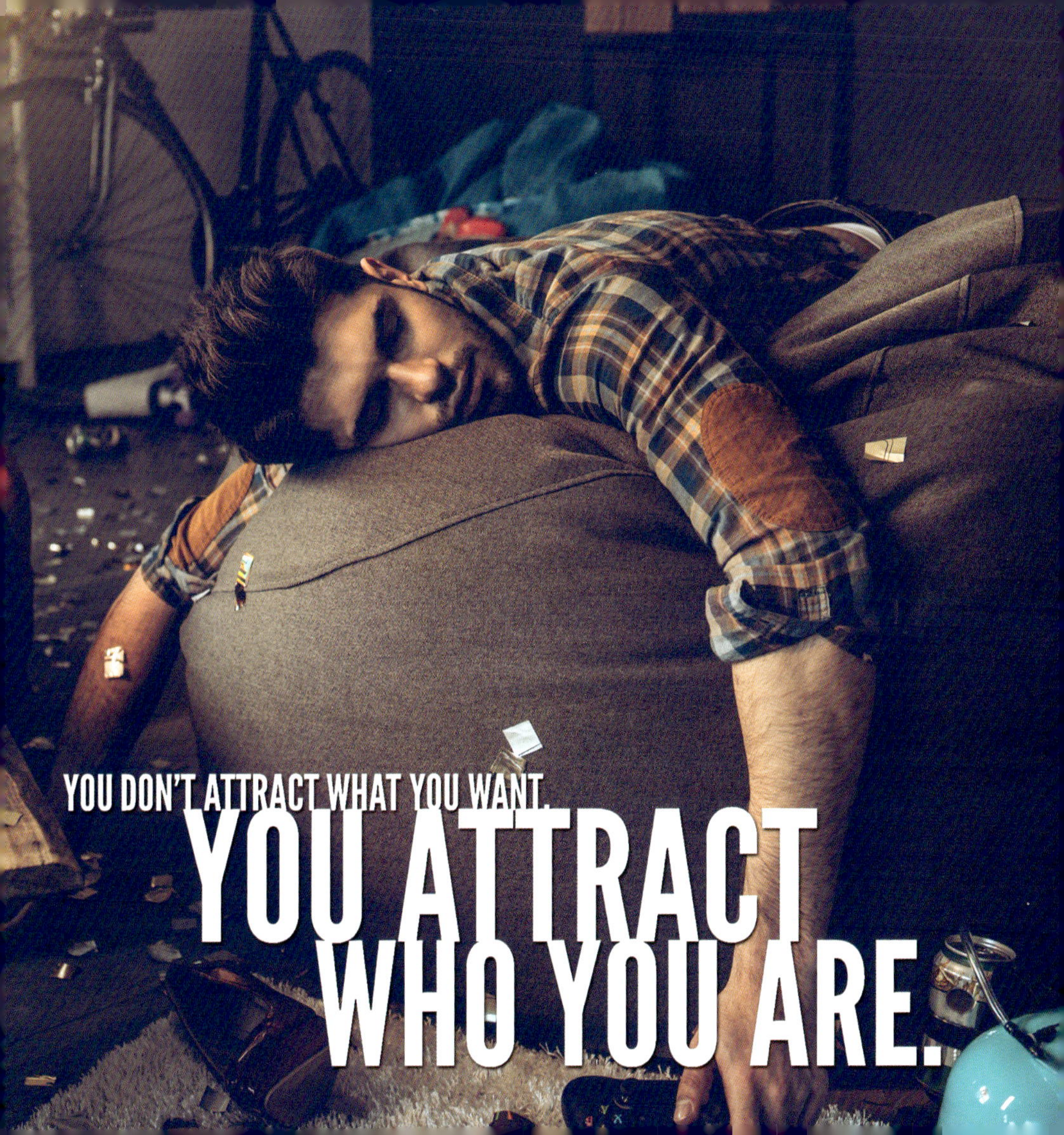
YOU DON'T ATTRACT WHAT YOU WANT.
YOU ATTRACT
WHO YOU ARE.

ADULTING

What will hurt you more
is not the sin you struggle with
but the sin you tolerate.

Little compromises that no one sees
will produce big failures that everyone sees.

CROSSING A LINE, WHETHER BY AN INCH OR A MILE, IS STILL OUT OF BOUNDS.

ADULTING

Your flesh's greatest weakness is the devil's strongest entry point.

You can't put yourself in a losing position and expect to win.

TEMPTATION IS WHERE PROPENSITY MEETS OPPORTUNITY.

ADULTING

The same devil that tempts you to sin
will beat you over the head
with condemnation after you've sinned.

As long as you continue
to be condemned about what you've done,
you're doomed to repeat it!

CONDEMNATION PUSHES YOU AWAY FROM GOD

ADULTING

It's not what you do when you sin that counts.
It's what you do after you sin.

It's not the size of your sin that counts
but the speed at which you run to Him.

CONVICTION
POINTS YOU
TO GOD

ADULTING

God's pile of mercy is always greater than your pile of sin.

Thanks to grace, we don't get what we deserve. We get what Jesus deserves.

Forget your sin, but never forget that you've been forgiven.

SMALL CHANGES
IN THE WORDS YOU SPEAK
WILL MAKE A BIG DIFFERENCE
IN THE LIFE YOU LIVE.

SPEAKING LIFE

SPEAKING LIFE

You receive the promises of God by believing and speaking them.

Before you can move into a successful future, a successful future must move into you.

don't use your words to describe your life.

use your words to design your life.

SPEAKING LIFE

Don't speak what you see.
Speak what you know.

Don't let reality become an anchor.
Let it propel you to the answer.

**DON'T SPEAK
WHAT YOU
EXPERIENCE.**

**SPEAK
WHAT YOU
EXPECT.**

HOLY BIBLE

SPEAKING LIFE

The words you speak are seeds
and will come back to you with a harvest,
good or bad.

You can't get a good crop
from a bad seed.

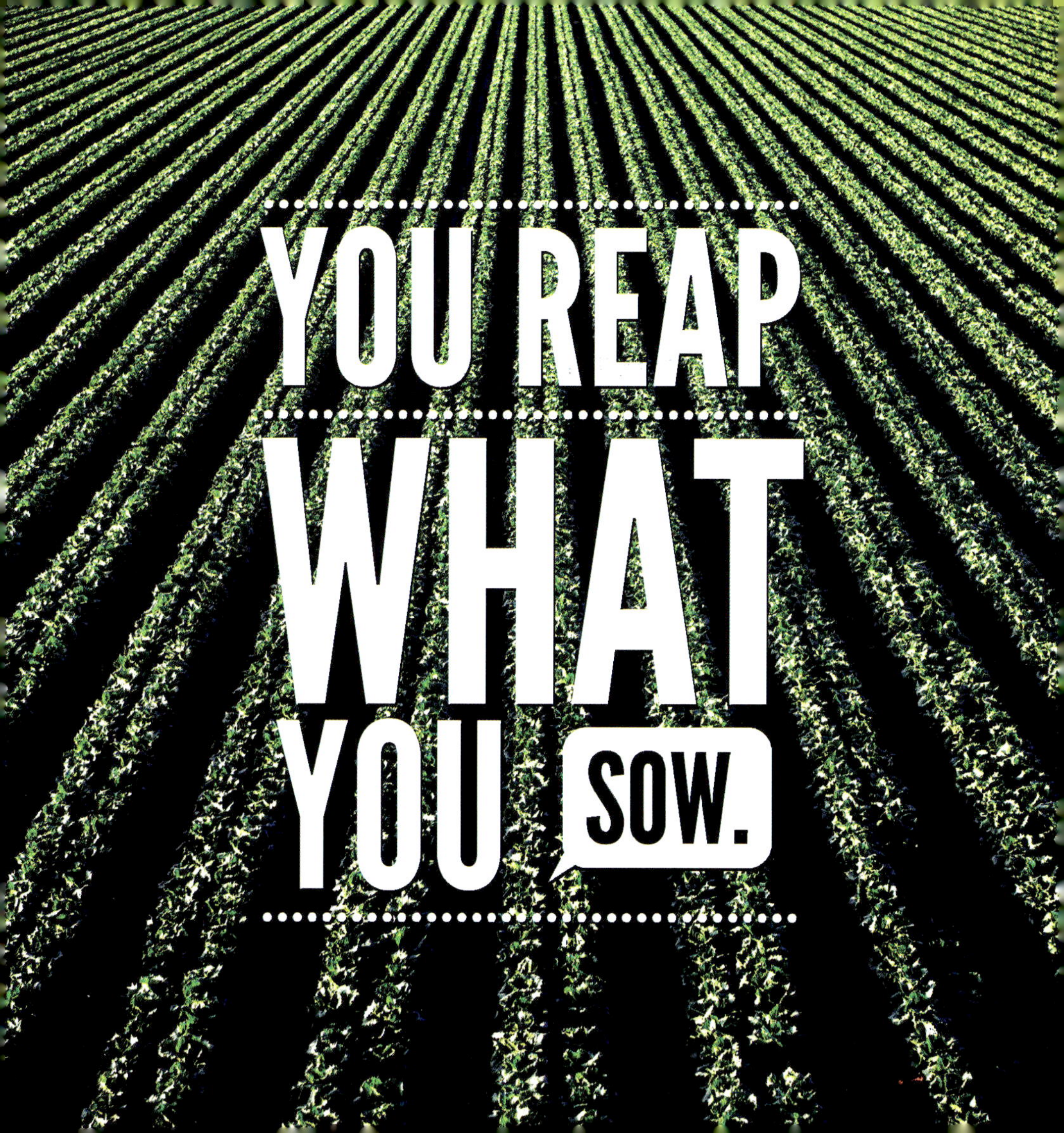
YOU REAP
WHAT
YOU
SOW.

SPEAKING LIFE

Don't call them like you see them.
Call them like God sees them!

Life is like a pair of binoculars.
Whatever you focus in on gets bigger.

MAGNIFY THE POSITIVE

-WHEN YOU CLEARLY-
SEE THE NEGATIVE

SPEAKING LIFE

You can't out-think the devil,
but you sure can out-speak him!
Curse what's in the way,
or it will continue to stay.

You don't need to tell God
about your big problem.
You need to tell your problem
about your big God.

DON'T JUST STARE AT YOUR MOUNTAINS.
SPEAK TO THEM!

SPEAKING LIFE

Problems aren't living things
unless you give them life with your words.

You get into trouble
when you speak out of your trouble.

when you give YOUR PROBLEMS YOUR VOICE, *you give them your* PERMISSION.

SPEAKING LIFE

Think like a victor.
Talk like a victor.

Don't respond from your condition.
Respond from your position.

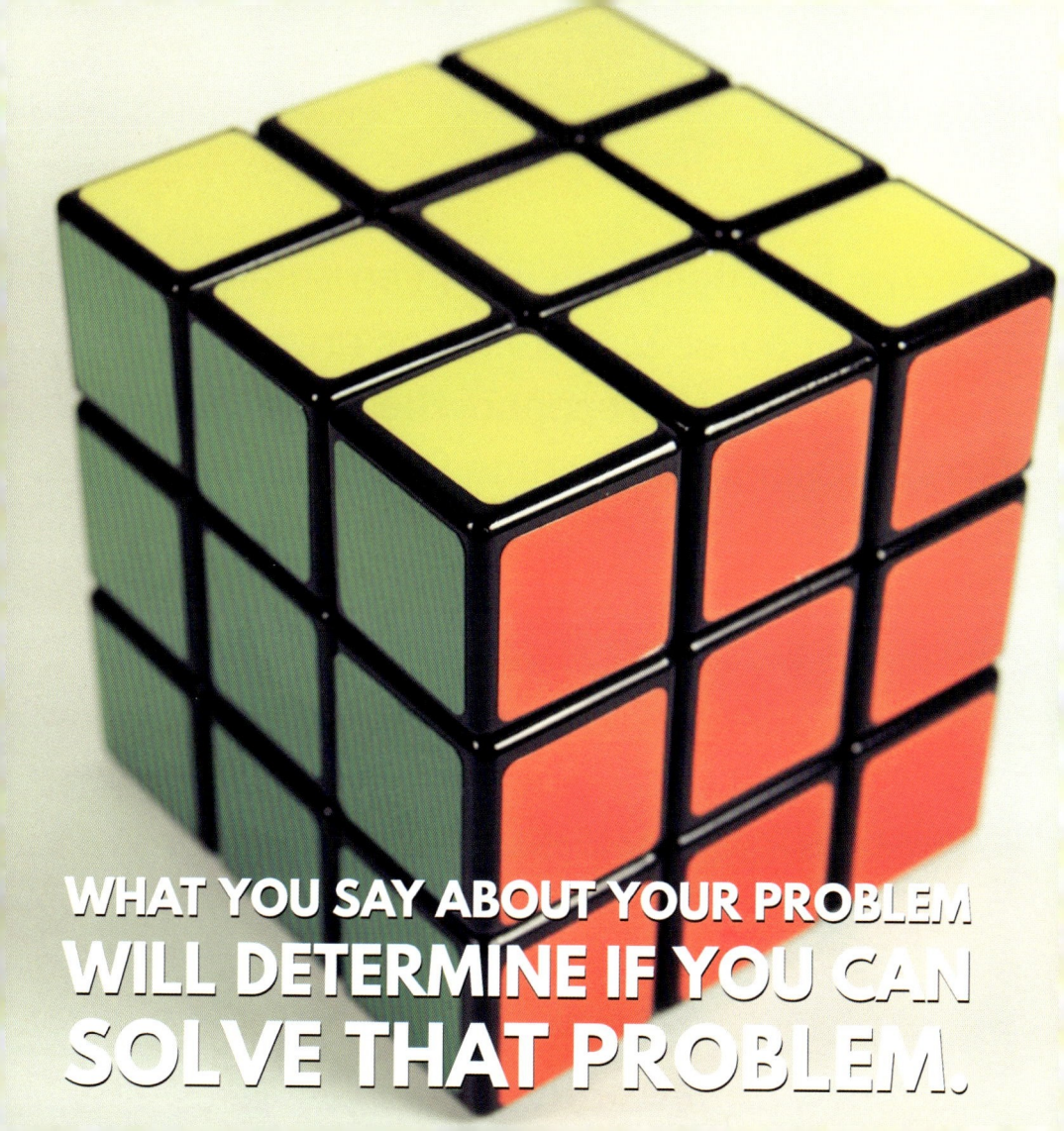

WHAT YOU SAY ABOUT YOUR PROBLEM WILL DETERMINE IF YOU CAN SOLVE THAT PROBLEM.

SPEAKING LIFE

The first thing you say in an emergency sets the course for your mess or your miracle. The quicker you respond, the more likely it is that your words will come from your emotions.

When the storms of life come, never rush to get ahold of your problem. First, get ahold of yourself!

EMOTIONS IN A CRISIS ARE LIKE THROWING GASOLINE ON A FIRE

SPEAKING LIFE

Complainers are not obtainers.

The words you speak
indicate the condition of your heart.

COMPLAINING IS CRITICIZING GOD'S ABILITY TO TAKE CARE OF YOU.

SPEAKING LIFE

If you want to change your feelings,
you must change your thoughts.
If you want to change your thoughts,
you must change your words.

Take the faith in your heart
and the words of your mouth
to overpower the doubt in your head.

SPEAKING WHAT YOU KNOW WILL EVENTUALLY CHANGE

SPEAKING LIFE

A bad mouth can ruin a good marriage.
A good mouth can heal a bad marriage.

If you want to change your marriage,
you must change how you talk to
and about your spouse.

YOU CAN'T HAVE A BAD MOUTH AND A GOOD MARRIAGE.

SPEAKING LIFE

In every man, there is a prince or a punk. Whoever you talk to will come out to play.

Talk to a contentious woman like a princess, and eventually she'll see the crown too.

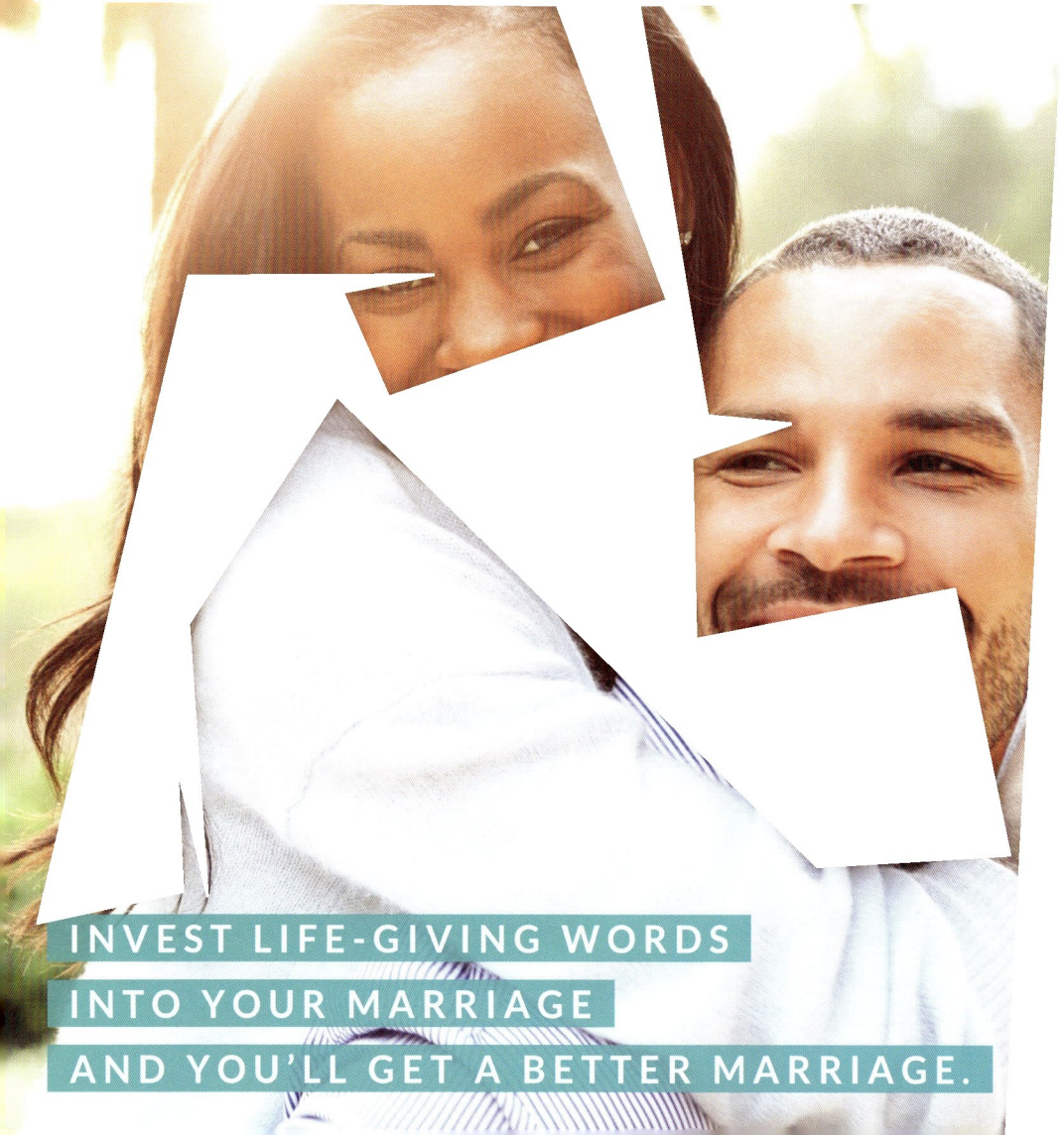

INVEST LIFE-GIVING WORDS INTO YOUR MARRIAGE AND YOU'LL GET A BETTER MARRIAGE.

SPEAKING LIFE

Repeating anything negative about a person when you are not a part of the problem or the solution is gossip.

Everything that you say must be true, but everything that is true does not need to be said.

WHEN YOU GOSSIP,

YOU'RE TALKING ABOUT GOD'S KIDS.

SPEAKING LIFE

You can heal a life in a sentence.
You can destroy a life in a sentence.

Believe that you have something valuable
to say about people.

Never underestimate the power of a kind word.

SPEAKING LIFE

You can't always choose
the people or things that come into your life.
But you can always choose
your attitude toward them.

The devil wants to use your mouth for death.
God wants to use your mouth for life.
You decide who gets to use it.

BE NICE!

THERE IS

COMING A TIME

WHEN ALL

YOU'LL HAVE LEFT

IS WHAT YOU'VE

GIVEN TO GOD.

MINISTRY

MINISTRY

If you can't serve people,
you can't teach people.

People won't care how much you know
until they know how much you care.

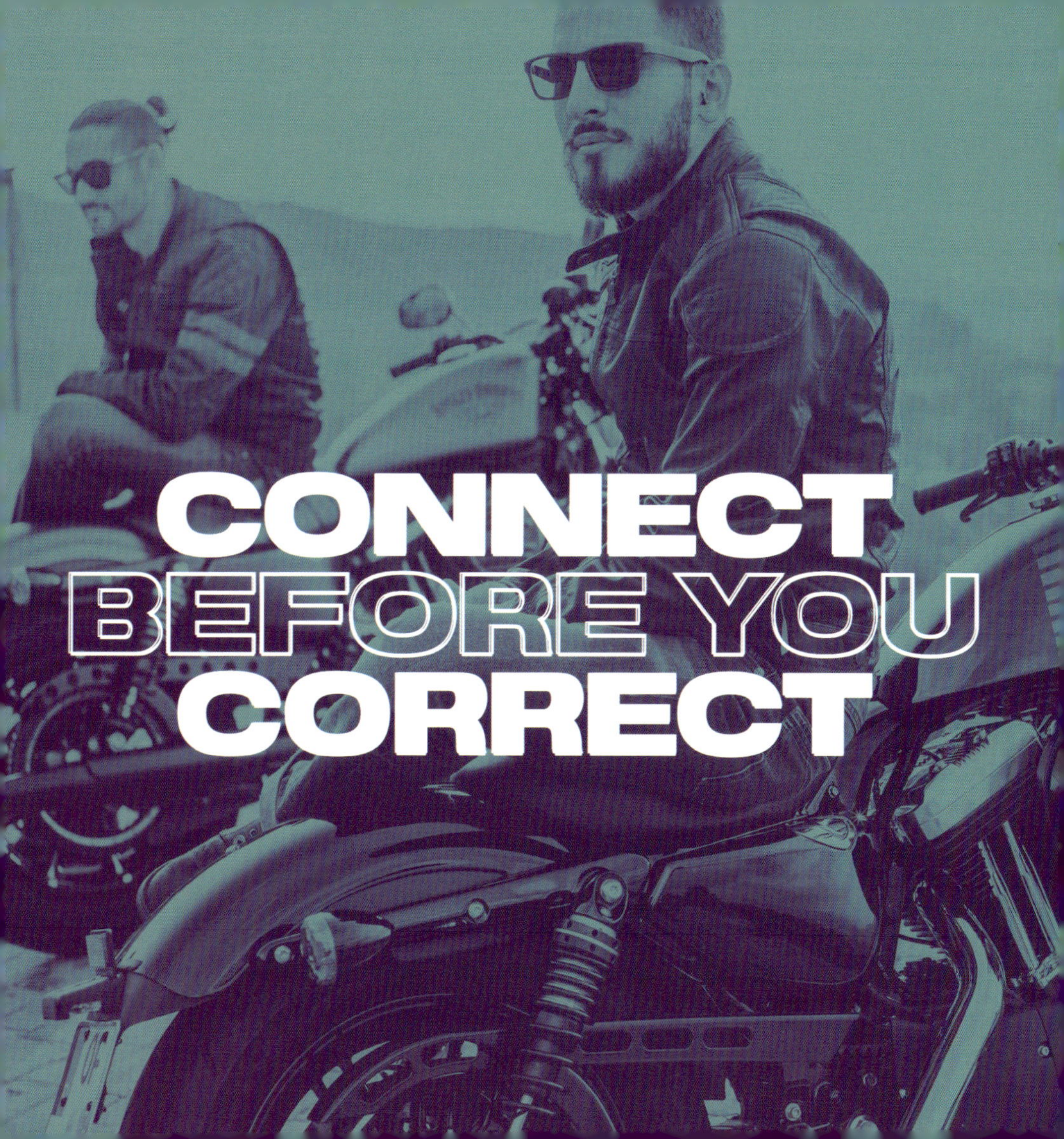
CONNECT
BEFORE YOU
CORRECT

MINISTRY

If you see a turtle on top of a fence post, you know it had help getting there!

Never try to succeed alone.

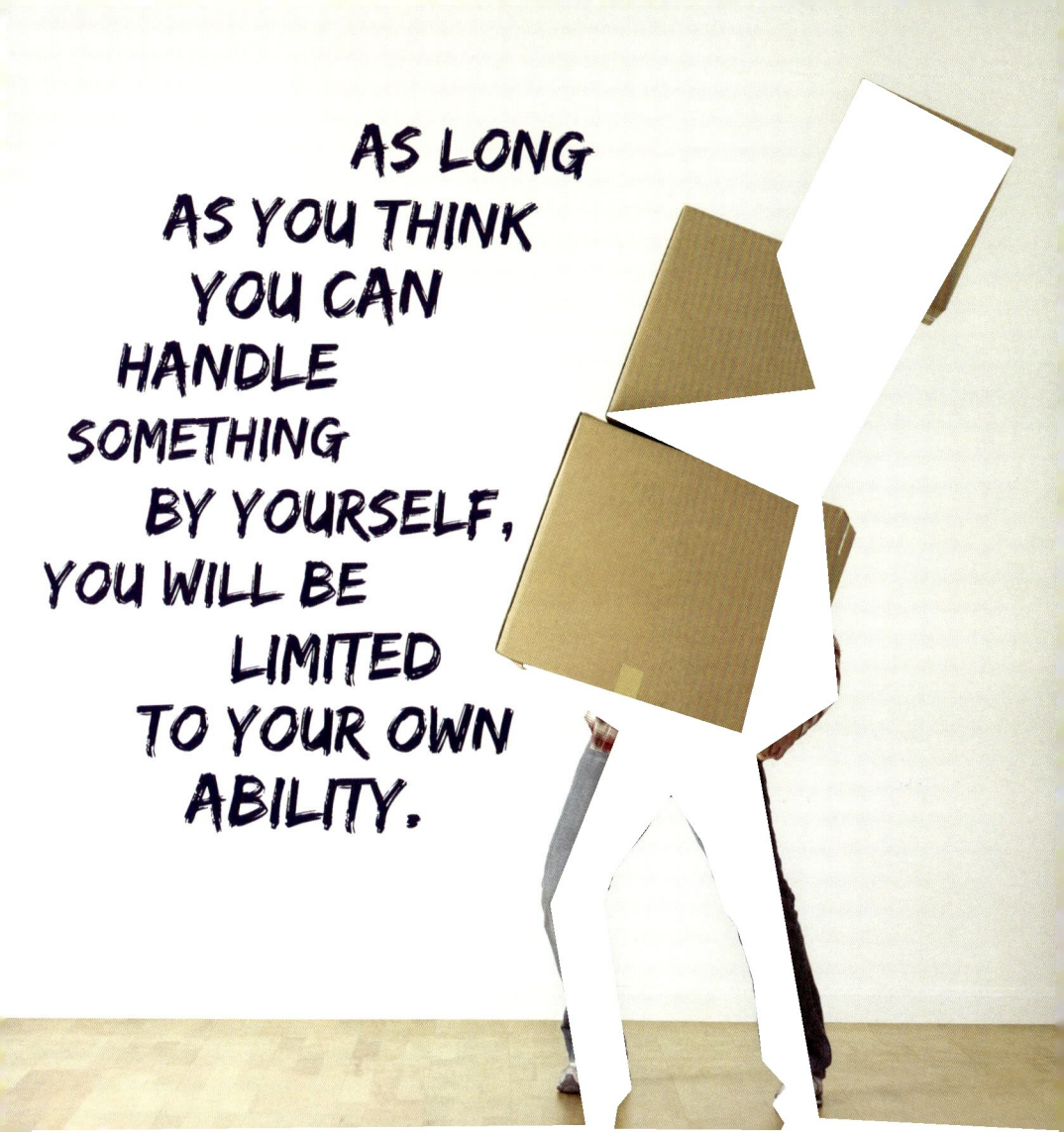

AS LONG AS YOU THINK YOU CAN HANDLE SOMETHING BY YOURSELF, YOU WILL BE LIMITED TO YOUR OWN ABILITY.

MINISTRY

Your gift will be developed privately before it is revealed publicly.

God will evaluate you in the small to see if you're ready for the big.

YOUR INITIAL ASSIGNMENT WILL NEVER MATCH THE SIZE OF YOUR VISION

MINISTRY

You will never find new levels of fruitfulness or influence without new levels of faithfulness and commitment.

You won't be rewarded by how many gifts you have but by your faithfulness to them.

YOU CAN'T EXECUTE A BIG VISION WITHOUT MAKING FAITHFUL DECISIONS.

MINISTRY

If you refuse to compromise, you will be rejected by many but promoted by One.

A big purpose will help you overcome the criticism of small people.

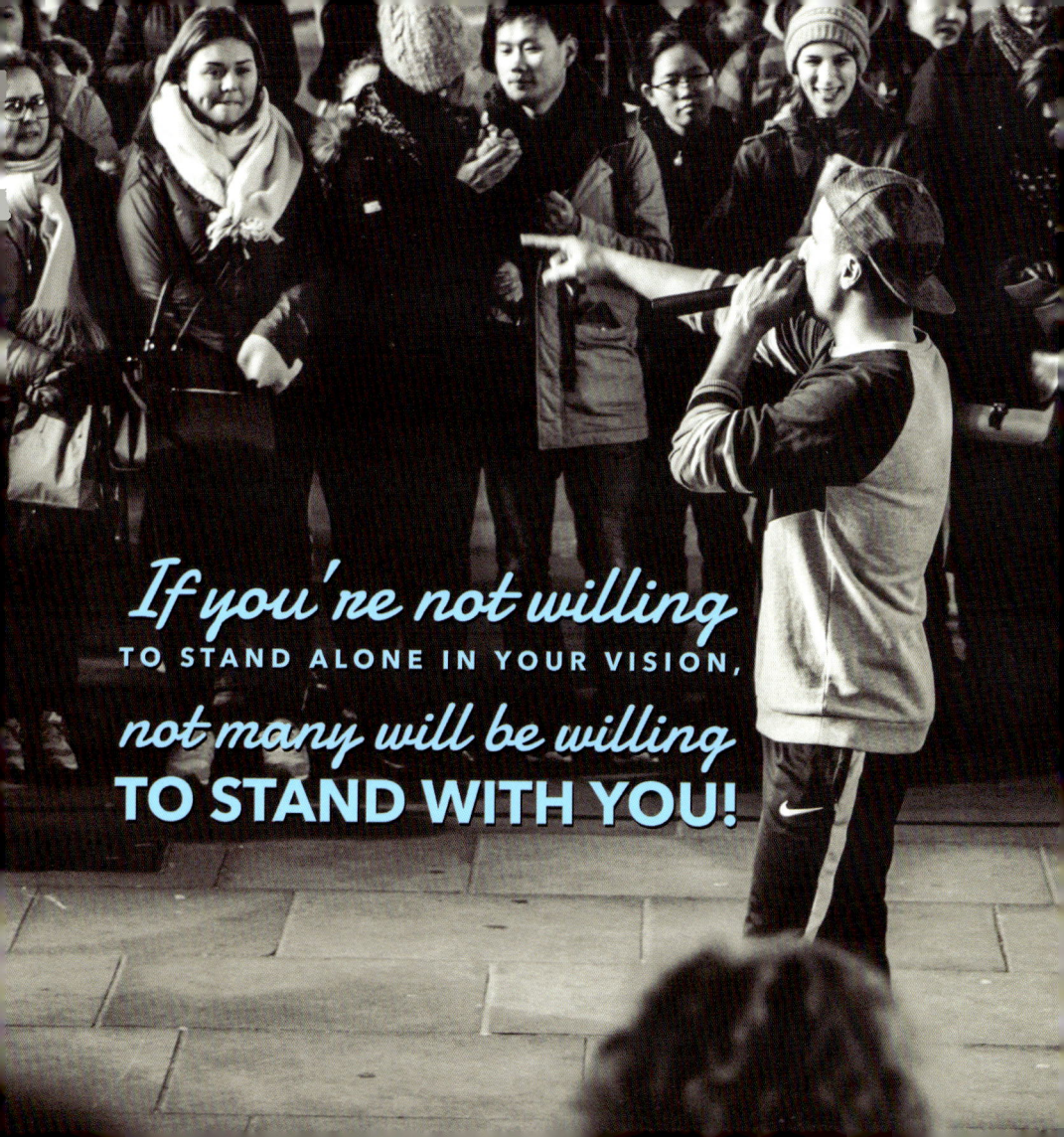

If you're not willing TO STAND ALONE IN YOUR VISION, *not many will be willing* **TO STAND WITH YOU!**

MINISTRY

God has not called you to activity but productivity.

Attempting too much will spread your motivation too thin.

GOOD LEADERS DON'T DO MORE.
THEY DO MORE OF WHAT IS MOST IMPORTANT.

MINISTRY

Your gift will get you in the room.
Your character will keep you in the room.

Don't hide behind your gift
as an excuse for not developing your character.

YOUR CHARACTER IS MORE IMPORTANT THAN YOUR GIFT.

MINISTRY

A leader must choose between popular and effective.

You can stand tall in principle and still stand by people.

WITH VISIBILITY COMES RESPONSIBILITY

MINISTRY

Stay connected to godly men and messages, but don't marry a method.

It's a good thing to be culturally relevant. You must do all you can to reach people . . . as long as you don't compromise.

NEVER SAY NEVER TO ANYTHING BUT COMPROMISE

MINISTRY

Be a living epistle, not a living tabloid.

You teach what you know,
but you impart who you are.

DON'T MAKE YOUR LIGHT SHINE.

let it shine.

MINISTRY

People may doubt what you say,
but they will usually believe what you do.

People will eventually cease to follow
those they cannot trust.

trust occurs when words and deeds are congruent.

MINISTRY

Anytime you move to a new level in God, people will find fault in you to soothe their conscience.

Those around you don't always have faith for what God has called you to do.

WHEN YOU BEGIN TO SHOW YOUR MARK ON THIS WORLD, MANY WILL SHOW UP WITH ERASERS.

MINISTRY

The more you do for God,
the more you'll be criticized by people.

If you're not ready to be criticized
for your obedience to God,
you're not ready to be used by God.

NEVER LET CRITICISM GO TO YOUR HEART.

MINISTRY

A servant pleases his master.
If you try to please men, they are your master!

You will only please 50% of the people,
no matter what you do.
Why not please God and 50% of the people?

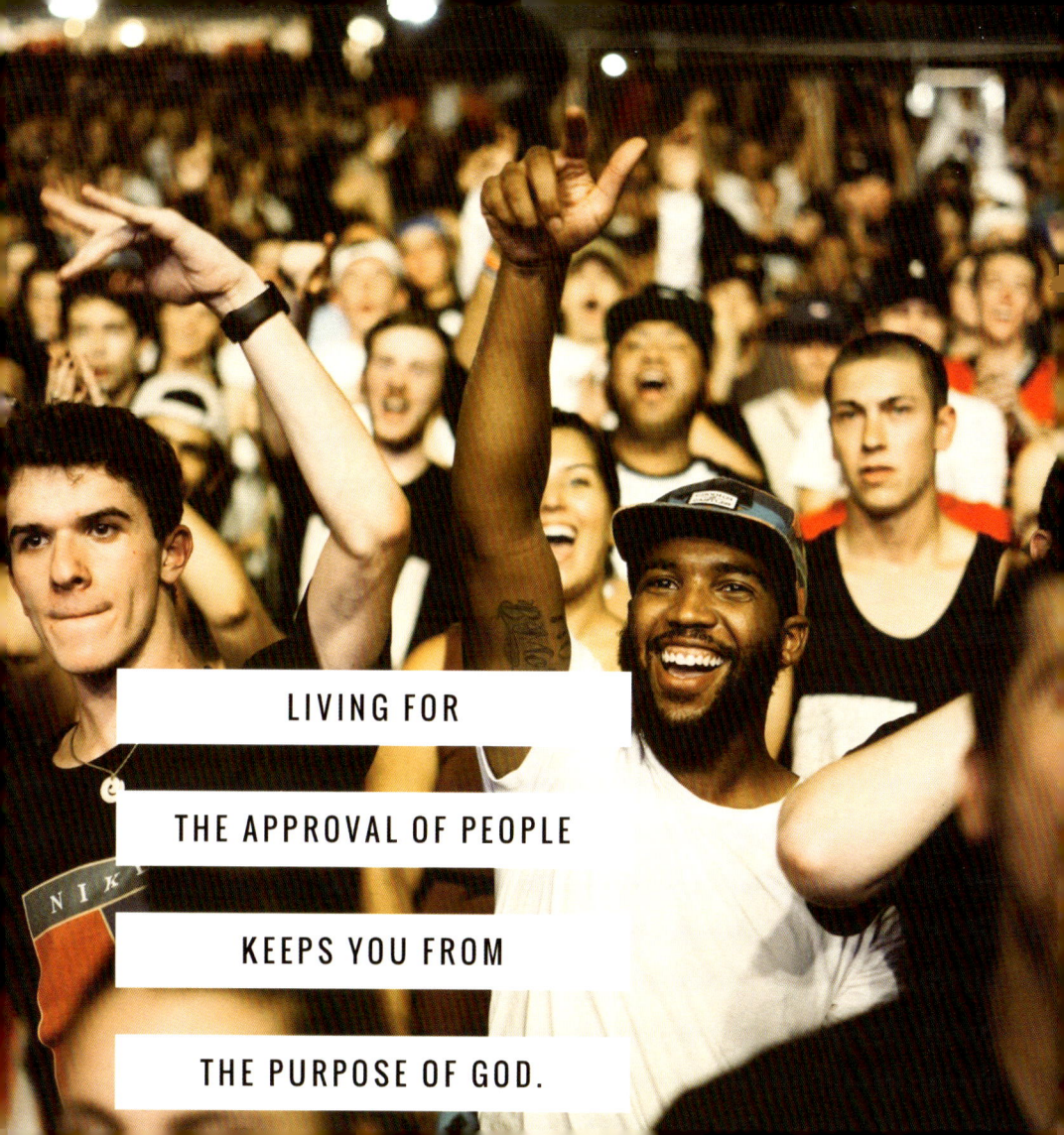

LIVING FOR THE APPROVAL OF PEOPLE KEEPS YOU FROM THE PURPOSE OF GOD.

MINISTRY

Go from being a "me too"
to doing what God has called *you* to do!

Dreams are either created or copied.
You'll never stay motivated
if your dream is not created.

THE HARDEST PERSON IN THIS WORLD TO BE

IS SOMEONE YOU'RE NOT.

MINISTRY

How much confidence people will have in you is directly related to how much of God they see in you.

The goal of Christianity is not ministry.
The goal of Christianity is intimacy.
Then, out of that intimacy flows true ministry.
If you don't understand this,
ministry becomes idolatry.

THE DEGREE TO WHICH YOU KNOW GOD WILL BE THE DEGREE TO WHICH YOU CAN MAKE HIM KNOWN.

FELLOWSHIP WITH JESUS IS YOUR HIGHEST CALLING.

DEVOTION

DEVOTION

**By putting God first,
you will act on life instead of reacting to life.**

**You always have time for
what you make time for.**

Go to the throne before you go to the phone.

DEVOTION

Thank God for revival,
but isn't it better to stay "vived"?

If you don't regularly come apart with Him,
your life will fall apart.

STAY STIRRED UP.
it's harder to start a fire
THAN IT IS TO KEEP ONE ABLAZE.

DEVOTION

He can turn your loss into a lesson.

He can turn your mess into a message.

GOD DIDN'T CAUSE YOUR PROBLEM BUT HE CAN TURN IT

DEVOTION

The area in which you worry most
is where you trust God the least.

Prayer takes your problem out of your hands
and puts it into God's hands.
So cast your care and leave it there.
Don't cast your care and sneak a peek!

NOTHING IS WORTH YOUR WORRY. EVERYTHING IS WORTH YOUR PRAYER.

DEVOTION

When you see yourself in Christ,
how God sees you because of
what Jesus has done for you,
you'll live your life based on your position
and not your condition.

The more you understand who you are in Him,
the better you'll get to know the Him you are in!

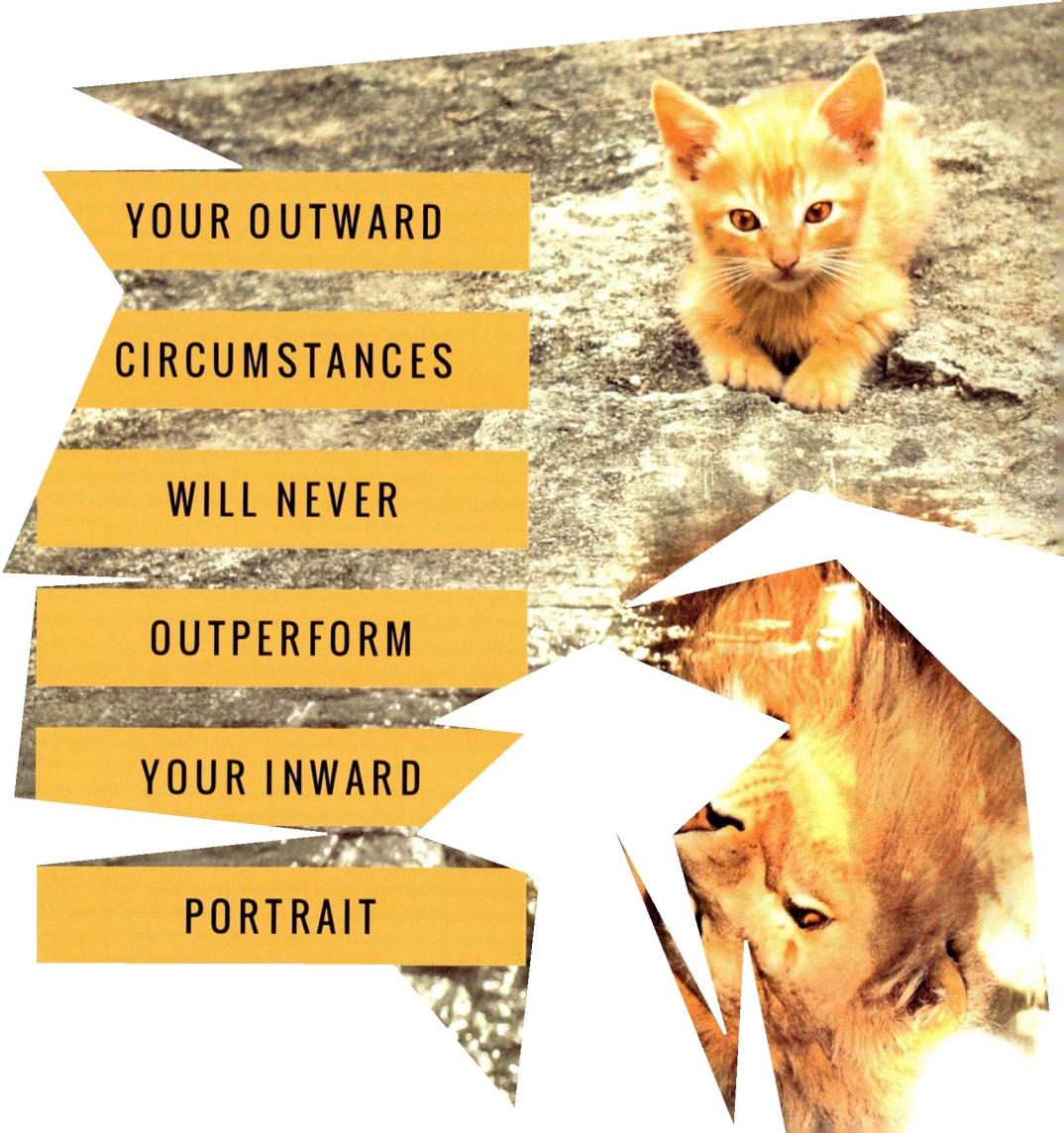

YOUR OUTWARD CIRCUMSTANCES WILL NEVER OUTPERFORM YOUR INWARD PORTRAIT

DEVOTION

Believe that God is working behind the scenes, even when you can't see any change.

Patience is the ability to
continue to do the same things
with no apparent difference
in your circumstances.

DON'T THROW AWAY WHAT YOU DO KNOW BECAUSE OF WHAT YOU DON'T KNOW

DEVOTION

Outcome is God's responsibility.
Obedience is your responsibility.

You don't have to understand completely
to obey immediately.

Real **SUCCESS** *comes from* **OBEDIENCE WITHOUT COMPROMISE.**

DEVOTION

You must change yourself,
but not by yourself.

God will never correct you
without giving you the power to change.

THE ROAD
TO GROWTH TRAVELS
THROUGH THE
CITY OF CHANGE.

DEVOTION

God loves you just the way you are.
However, He loves you too much
to leave you that way.

God will not let you get away with low decisions
because you have such a high calling.

GOD'S NOT ABOUT REPLACING DAMAGED PEOPLE. HE'S ABOUT FIXING THEM.

DEVOTION

Knowledge is the taking in of God's Word.
Wisdom is the putting out of God's Word.

The less wisdom you have,
the more miracles you'll need.
The more wisdom you have,
the fewer miracles you'll need.

WISDOM IS LIVING IN A WAY THAT WORKS

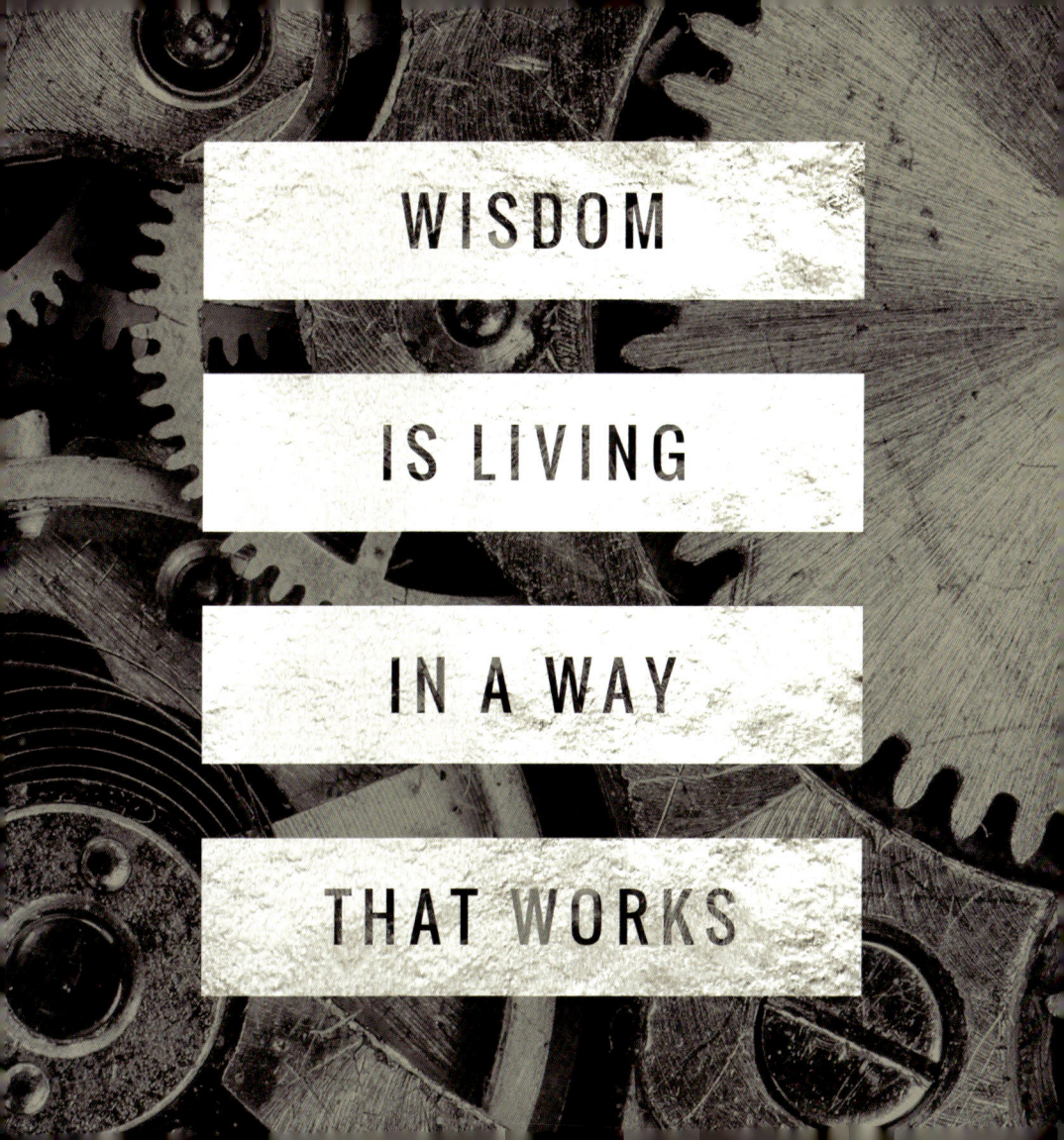

DEVOTION

Tithing, fasting, praying, and living a holy life do not initiate God's love for you.
They are a response to God's love for you.

It's not that you need to love Him more.
It's that you need to receive more of His love.

*God's love initiates.
Our love responds.*

GOD LOVES YOU
AS IF YOU WERE
THE ONLY PERSON
IN THIS WORLD
TO LOVE!

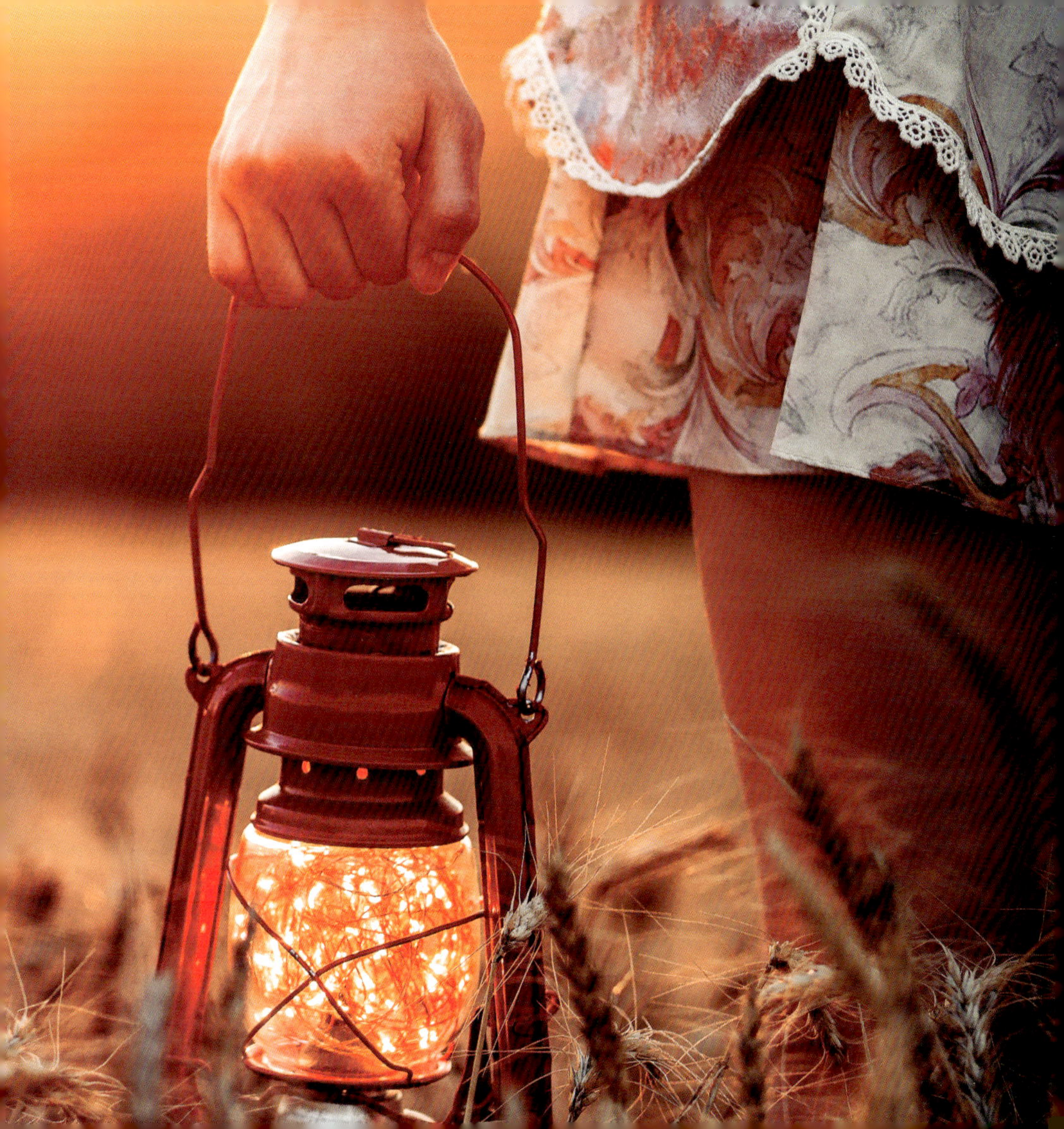

HOW TO START THE MOST IMPORTANT RELATIONSHIP OF YOUR LIFE

Shark fishing is my hobby. I use a kayak to paddle my bait hundreds of yards into the ocean, then paddle back and fish from the shore. Some time ago, I was in the midst of a four-hour battle with a very large shark, and a crowd had gathered from around the beach to see what I was going to reel in. A man in the crowd struck up a conversation with me while I was battling this shark. He asked me what I did for a living, and I told him I was a pastor.

When people discover that I am a pastor, I get a wide variety of responses. This man's response was unusual. He simply blurted out with disdain, "Well, I hate organized religion!" I replied, "Me too." He was visibly shocked, so I continued. I asked, "You know who else hates organized religion?" Before he could respond, I surprised him further and said, "Jesus!" I had this fellow's undivided attention, and I hope that I now have yours as well.

You see, Christianity is not about religion. It is about a relationship with a loving, heavenly Father through His one Son, Jesus Christ. I believe that you have a figurative homing beacon placed on the inside of you by the One who created you: God. A spiritual hole, if you will, that can only be filled by Him.

Before I entered into a relationship with Jesus, I tried to fill that hole with women, alcohol, and fighting. It was fun for a while, but when the fun was over, and the things I tried to fill that vacuum with came crashing down around me, I still had that homing beacon on the inside of me. My heavenly Father was gently, patiently, and ever so lovingly calling me home.

Maybe you can sense the emptiness on the inside of you and the loving call of your heavenly Father, imploring you to come home. Why not surrender your life to Him and find the joy, peace, and purpose you've been looking for all of your life? Why not start the most important relationship of your life? It's so simple, but life transforming.

Please pray this prayer with me. Repeat it out loud, but mean it from your heart. I discovered a long time ago that when you reach out to God from your heart, He will always reach back to you with His love.

Pray this simple prayer with me now:

"Father God, I come to you now. Sin, I turn my back on you. Jesus, I turn to you now. I believe you died on the cross just for me. I believe you were raised from the dead just for me. Come into my heart, and be my Lord. I surrender my life to you today. I enter into relationship with you today!"

If you prayed that prayer, please contact us here at Joy Church, and let us know that you started the most important relationship of your life. We want to respect your privacy and dignity, but we also want to give you some information to help you walk out this new relationship in a life-giving way!

You can email us at mail@joychurchinternational.org or give us a call at 615-773-5252. You can write to us at Joy Church, P.O. Box 247, Mount Juliet, TN, 37121.

If you live in or are visiting the Nashville/Mount Juliet, TN area, we would love to invite you to join us for one of our upcoming services. For more information and directions, please visit our website at www.joychurch.net. We look forward to hearing from you!

Please remember that God loves you as if you were the only person in this world to love!

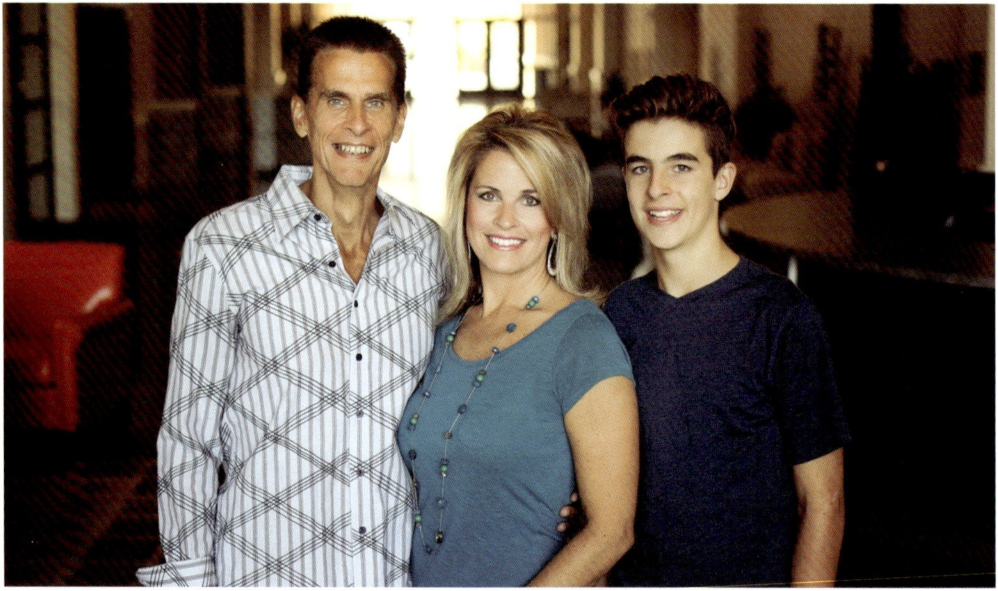

ABOUT THE AUTHOR

Jim Frease is the founder and senior pastor of Joy Church in Mount Juliet, Tennessee, and founder and president of World Changers Bible Institute (WCBI). He is also the founder of Joy Ministerial Exchange (JME), a ministerial organization designed to impart to pastors across the country.

Jim emphasizes a relationship with Jesus Christ, not religion; the Word of God, not tradition; and he emphasizes enjoying life, not enduring it. He teaches not just what to do, but how.

Jim and his wife Anne have been married since 1990 and deeply love their son, Johnathan. Jim loves spending time with his family, and he enjoys Ohio State football and fishing. Anne loves to shop. Sometimes, they compromise and shop at Bass Pro.

Most importantly, Jim and Anne are deeply in love with the Lord Jesus Christ and are completely committed to His Word. As they minister, they do so with humor, joy (Nehemiah 8:10), and integrity (Psalm 26:11), propelling the listener to a greater intimacy with Jesus.

JOY church

Tired of enduring life? Start enjoying life!

Based out of Mt. Juliet, Tennessee, Joy Church is a rapidly growing, multi-generational, multicultural church with people from almost every denominational background—including those with no church background at all.

At Joy Church, we don't believe in organized religion; we believe in organized *relationship* with God the Father through His Son, Jesus Christ. We are not about tradition, but the liberating Word of God. We are not about enduring life—we are about *enjoying* life!

For more information, please visit us online at www.joychurch.net.

WINNING WITH WISDOM

PEARLS OF WISDOM FOR YOUR NEXT RIGHT DECISION